CLARINET

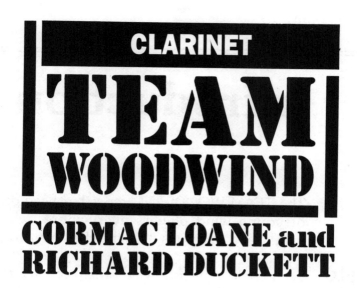

TEAM WOODWIND

CORMAC LOANE and RICHARD DUCKETT

International Music Publications Limited

Introduction

The TEAM WOODWIND series has been designed to meet the needs of young wind players everywhere, whether lessons are given individually, in groups or in the classroom.

Musical variety

Each book contains a wide variety of musical styles, from the Baroque and Classical eras to film, folk, jazz and Latin American. In addition there are original pieces and studies, technical exercises and scales, progressing from the beginner stage to approximately Grade IV standard of the *Associated Board of the Royal Schools of Music*. Furthermore TEAM WOODWIND offers material suitable for mixed wind ensemble as well as solos with piano accompaniment.

Ensemble pieces

All TEAM WOODWIND books contain corresponding pages of music which can be played together in harmony. Beginners are thus given early ensemble experience and the opportunity to share lessons with other players, whether they play treble or bass clef, B flat, C or E flat pitched instruments, or even guitar or keyboards.

The ensemble material in the TEAM WOODWIND series integrates with the same material in TEAM BRASS and thus offers exciting possibilities for mixed instrumental lessons, concerts and assemblies.

Study options

The TEAM WOODWIND series is not a 'method'. It is a selection of primer music from which the teacher can select a suitably graded course for each pupil. This allows for variation in concentration threshold and tempo of progression. There are also several choices of progressive path the pupil can follow. Study options appear at the foot of appropriate pages.

GCSE skills

In addition to fostering musical literacy, Rhythm Grids and Play By Ear lines provide early opportunities for composition and improvisation. This aspect of TEAM WOODWIND can be a useful starting point for these elements in the GCSE examination course now followed in many secondary schools.

Comprehensive notes on the use of this series, scores of ensemble pieces and piano accompaniments are given in the ACCOMPANIMENTS book.

Note:

In some of the earlier pieces in the TEAM WOODWIND solo books the key signatures appear with bracketted sharps or flats. Whereas each key signature is academically correct, the brackets serve to indicate sharps or flats that have not as yet been introduced to the player. These sharps or flats do not appear in the exercise or piece. On the concert pitch cue line of the piano arrangements, however, the key signatures are indicated in the usual way.

Team Woodwind Ensemble

TEAM WOODWIND ensemble material has been specially written so that it can be played by almost any combination of wind instruments that the teacher is likely to encounter. The pieces are basically for duet, to which can be added independent (and inessential) 3rd and 4th parts if required.

The related ensemble parts for the duets in this book will be found in the BASSOON book, and in the Supplement to the SAXOPHONE book as well as in the Supplement which accompanies this book. The ensemble parts for clarinet are for both B flat and C clarinets.

This book contains ensemble material relating to the duets in TEAM WOODWIND for FLUTE. Relevant third parts are to be found in the Supplement provided. Also, the B flat/C clarinet ensemble material integrates fully with the ensemble material in the TEAM BRASS books. TEAM WOODWIND and TEAM BRASS ensemble can therefore be combined for both small wind/brass groups or for full-sized wind orchestras.

All the ensemble material is graded to match the lesson material. The ensemble pieces may easily be located by following the direction at the foot of the appropriate lesson page. Scores for all ensemble material and more extensive notes appear in the ACCOMPANIMENTS book.

The following symbols have been used to provide an immediate visual identification:

  Pieces with piano accompaniment

  Part of an ensemble arrangement for all C, B flat and E flat instruments (scores included in ACCOMPANIMENTS book)

  Pieces playable by clarinet and flute in unison, thirds or harmony.

Because the ensemble pieces provide a meeting point for players who are at various stages of development, these pieces may include technical elements (new notes, rhythms, etc) which are not in fact introduced until some pages later.

Edited by BARRIE CARSON TURNER

Piano accompaniments by GEOFFRY RUSSELL-SMITH and BARRIE CARSON TURNER

INTERNATIONAL MUSIC PUBLICATIONS would like to thank the following publishers for permission to use arrangements of their copyright material in TEAM WOODWIND.
IN THE MOOD - Words by JOE GARLAND, Music by ANDY RAZAF
© 1939 & 1991 Shapiro Bernstein & Co. Inc., USA
Sub-published by Peter Maurice Music Co. Ltd., London WC2H 0EA
I COULD HAVE DANCED ALL NIGHT - Words by ALAN JAY LERNER, Music by FREDERICK LOEWE
© 1956 & 1991 Alan Jay Lerner and Frederick Loewe
Chappell & Co. Inc., New York, NY, publisher and owner of allied rights throughout the world.
By arrangement with Lowal Corporation. Chappell Music Ltd., London W1Y 3FA
DON'T SIT UNDER THE APPLE TREE (WITH ANYONE ELSE BUT ME) - Words and Music by LEW BROWN, CHARLIE TOBIAS and SAM H. STEPT
© 1942 & 1991 Robbins Music Corporation USA
Redwood Music Ltd., London NW1 8BD/Memory Lane Music Ltd., London WC2H 8NA/EMI United Partnership Ltd., London WC2H 0EA
STRANGER ON THE SHORE - Words by ROBERT MELLIN, Music by ACKER BILK
© 1962 & 1991 EMI Music Publishing Ltd, London WC2H 0EA
MOONLIGHT SERENADE - Words by MITCHELL PARISH, Music by GLENN MILLER
© 1939 & 1991 Robbins Music Corporation, USA
EMI United Partnership Ltd., London WC2H 0EA
MOOD INDIGO - Words and Music by DUKE ELLINGTON, IRVING MILLS and ALBANY BIGARD
© 1931 & 1991 Gotham Music Service Inc, USA
Sub-published by EMI Music Publishing Ltd., London WC2H 0EA
WHAT A WONDERFUL WORLD - Words and Music by GEORGE DAVID WEISS & BOB THIELE
© 1967 & 1991 Herald Square Music Company, USA
Carlin Music Corp., London NW1 8BD
WATERMELON MAN - Music by HERBIE HANCOCK, Words by JIMI HENDRIX
© 1962 & 1991 Hancock Music Co.
B. Feldman & Co. Ltd., London WC2H 0EA
BLOWIN' IN THE WIND - Words and Music by BOB DYLAN
© 1963 & 1991 Witmark & Sons, USA
Warner Chappell Music Ltd., London W1Y 3FA
EDELWEISS (From THE SOUND OF MUSIC) - Lyrics by OSCAR HAMMERSTEIN II, Music by RICHARD RODGERS
Copyright © 1959 by Richard Rodgers and Oscar Hammerstein II
Copyright Renewed.
This arrangement Copyright © 1991 by WILLIAMSON MUSIC CO.
WILLIAMSON MUSIC owner of publication and allied rights throughout the world.
International Copyright Secured   All Rights Reserved
LOVE ME TENDER - Words and Music by VERA MATSON & ELVIS PRESLEY
© 1956 & 1991 Elvis Presley Music Inc., USA
Carlin Music Corp., London NW1 8BD
LITTLE DONKEY - Words and Music by ERIC BOSWELL
© 1959 & 1991 Chappell Music Ltd., London W1Y 3FA
THE PINK PANTHER - by HENRY MANCINI
© 1963 & 1991 United Artists Music Co. Inc., USA
EMI United Partnership Ltd., London WC2H 0EA
OVER THE RAINBOW - Words by E. Y. HARBURG, Music by HAROLD ARLEN
© 1938 & 1991 Leo Feist Inc., USA
EMI United Partnership Ltd., London WC2H 0EA
SWEET GEORGIA BROWN - Words and Music by BEN BERNIE, KENNETH CASEY & MACEO PINKARD
© 1925 & 1991 Remick Music Corp, USA
Sub-published by Francis Day & Hunter Ltd., London WC2H 0EA and Redwood Music Ltd., London NW1 8BD
STAR WARS Main Title - by JOHN WILLIAMS
© 1977 & 1991 Fox Fanfare Music Inc.
Warner Chappell Music Ltd., London W1Y 3FA

Sincere thanks are extended to the following people whose criticism, advice and help in various ways have been invaluable.
KEITH ALLEN, Head of Music Services for the City of Birmingham Education Department.
PHILIP BROOKES, Bassoonist.
PETER BULLOCK, Clarinet Teacher, Derbyshire County Education Department.
RICHARD REAKES, Oboe Teacher, City of Birmingham Education Department.
DAVID ROBINSON, Woodwind Teacher, Kirklees Education Department.
JULIE SCHRODER, Flute Teacher, City of Birmingham Education Department.
ALISON WHATLEY, Oboe Teacher, City of Birmingham Education Department.
And also to the many pupils who have worked with the TEAM WOODWIND books in transcript form.
First Published 1991

Cover Design: Ian Barrett / David Croft
Cover Photography: Ron Goldby
Production: Stephen Clark / David Croft
Reprographics: Cloverleaf
Instruments photographed by courtesy of Vincent Bach International Ltd., London.
Typeset by Cromwell Typesetting & Design Ltd., London / Printed in England by Halstan & Co. Ltd.

TEAM WOODWIND: Clarinet
ISBN 0 86359 783 1 / Order Ref: 17533 / 215-2-654

Lesson diary & practice chart

Date (week commencing)	Enter number of minutes practised.							Teacher indicates which pages to study.
	Mon	Tue	Wed	Thur	Fri	Sat	Sun	

What to do with the reed and mouthpiece

Wet the reed by putting it in your mouth.
Place the ligature onto the mouthpiece.
Tighten the screws so that the reed is kept
firmly in place on the mouthpiece.

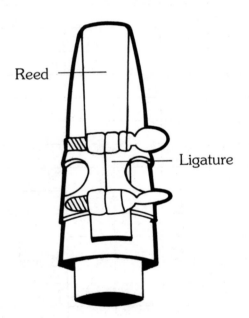

Reed

Ligature

Look in a mirror to check that you are
holding the clarinet the way your teacher
tells you.

Getting Started

How to put the Clarinet together

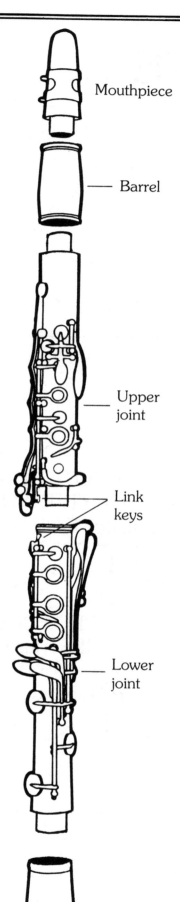

Mouthpiece

Barrel

Upper joint

Link keys

Lower joint

Bell

1. Hold the upper joint in your right hand and press down the rings. This will raise the link key (see picture).

2. Now take the lower joint in your left hand and carefully twist the two joints together. Make sure the two link keys are lined up (see picture).

3. Gently twist the bell onto the bottom of the lower joint.

4. Put the mouthpiece and the barrel together.

5. Twist the mouthpiece and barrel onto the top of the upper joint.

All of the material on this page can be played harmonically in 3rds with page 2 in the FLUTE book, as an aid to group teaching.

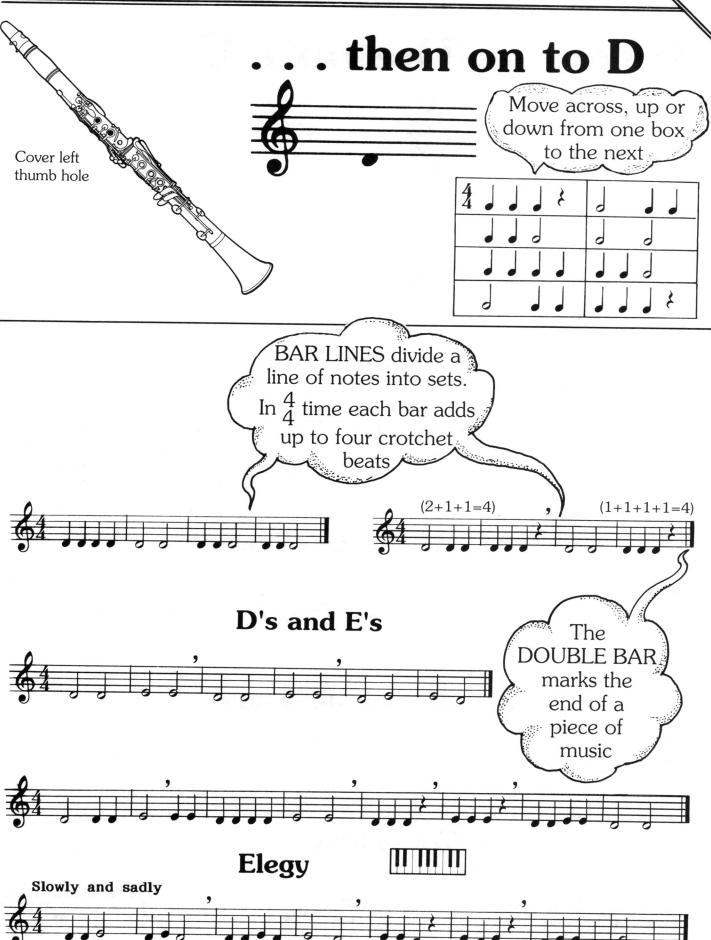

All of the material on this page can be played harmonically in 3rds with page 3 in the FLUTE book.

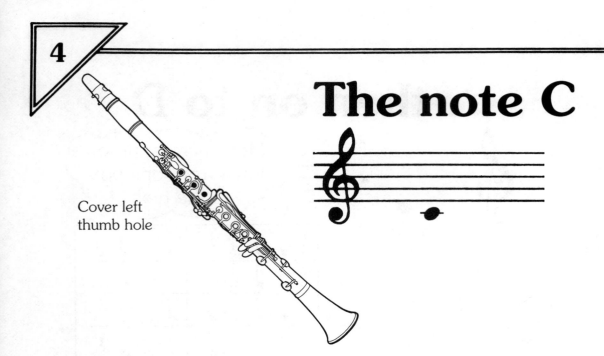

Cover left thumb hole

The note C

C, D and E march

A SEMIBREVE (or WHOLE-NOTE) lasts for FOUR beats

Merrily we roll along

Traditional

Au clair de la lune

Traditional

Tricky tune

■ Tunes carrying the symbol ⬭⬭ can be played in unison, thirds or harmony with the same tunes which appear in the FLUTE SUPPLEMENT.

The note F

Cover left thumb hole only

Flowing

3RDS

Walking

3RDS

Sort 'em out

March tempo

The note G

No thumb

Eudoxia

Traditional

Welsh tune

Traditional

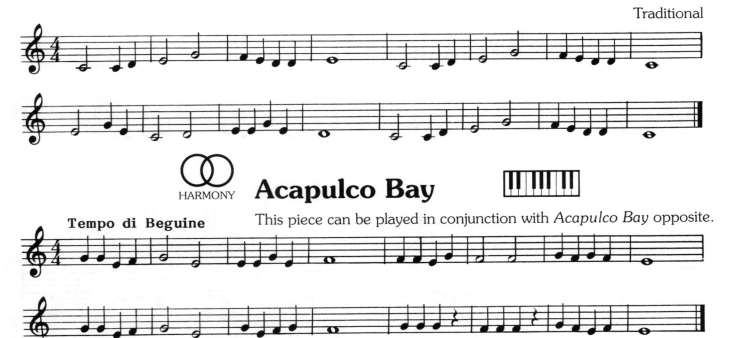

HARMONY

Acapulco Bay

This piece can be played in conjunction with *Acapulco Bay* opposite.

Tempo di Beguine

■ For related ensemble material see pages 14 and 15. Proceed to further material on pages 7-9; or Low B on page 10; or A on page 16.

Five-note patterns

Intervals

Step round

Acapulco Bay

HARMONY

This piece can be played in conjunction with *Acapulco Bay* opposite.

Tempo di Beguine

$\frac{3}{4}$ time

Every bar adds up to three crotchets

Slow waltz

Four bar question phrase, A   Four bar answer phrase, B

This means 'rest' for 4 whole bars- so count ① 2 3 ② 2 3 ③ 2 3 ④ 2 3 and then play from bar 5

A DOTTED MINIM lasts for THREE beats

Les ballons

Gently and dreamily

getting slower

HARMONY **Round lullaby**

(1)   (2)

■ Proceed to B on page 10; or A on page 16; or quavers on page 17.

More tunes using C, D, E, F and G

Shepherds' hey

Traditional

Old woman, old woman

Traditional

Barcarolle

JACQUES OFFENBACH
(1819-1880)

Jazzily

Continue

Brightly

Continue

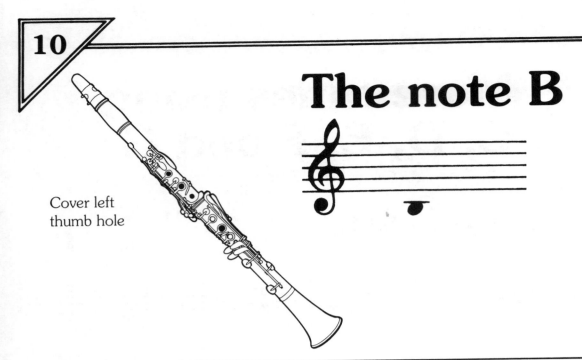

The note B

Cover left
thumb hole

Sharks!

B with C, D and E

HARMONY

One man and his dog

Traditional

■ For related ensemble material see pages 14 & 15.

Low A

Cover left thumb hole

The note low G

Cover left thumb hole

UNISON

Go and tell aunt Rhody

Traditional

■ Related ensemble material for Low A on page 37; extra material using Low A and G on page 12.

More tunes using low B, A and G

Jingle bells

Traditional

Good King Wenceslas

Traditional

Yankee Doodle

Traditional

Canon

THOMAS TALLIS (c. 1505-1585)

(1)   (2)   (3)   (4)

*Suggested alternative rhythm may be used.

Slurs

Slur round

Morning

EDVARD GRIEG
(1843-1907)

German tune

Duet

Lullaby

Duet

Tunes carrying the symbol can be played with tunes of the same name, on the same numbered pages in the other TEAM WOODWIND and TEAM BRASS books.

Tied notes

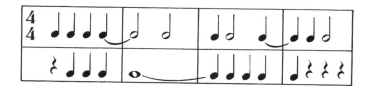

A minim tied to a crotchet lasts for 3 beats.

A crotchet tied to a crotchet lasts for 2 beats.

A semibreve tied to a crotchet lasts for 5 beats, and so on.

Don't be late!

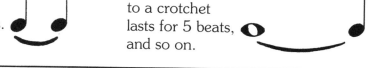

Canzonetta

Duet

Fast
(Polyphonic texture)

soft
COUNT
① 2 3 4   ② 2 3 4

soft

Compose a part for tambour or tambourine

A (Homophonic texture)

loud

loud

■ More tied notes on pages 20 & 21. Preparatory rounds on pages 7, 8 & 13.

The note A

No thumb

Pattern

Phrase A   Phrase B   Phrase A repeated   Phrase C
1   2   3   4

Slow round

(1)   (2)

play by ear

Slowly   Continue   Merrily   Continue

■ Proceed to Quavers, page 17; or F♯ page 18; or B♭ page 22. For related ensemble material see pages 20 & 21.

Quavers

The note F#

No thumb

The SHARP raises the pitch of a note by one semitone

Compose your own piece about a bird or animal – or one of the seasons

The cuckoo

HARMONY

Composed by
ten-year old
Edward Duckett

The cuckoo ruturns in spring. . .

loud

Fine

. . . and departs in autumn . . . . .

soft

D.C. al Fine

Watch out for F's which are not sharp

play by ear

Jazzily

Continue

Merrily

Continue

The key signature of G major

Scale and arpeggio of G major

Unto us a boy is born

Traditional

Austrian holiday

F/F♯ Study

Regal fanfare

*Fanfare part for timpani (or bass drum and tenor drum) and cymbals

¢ means TWO MINIM BEATS in each bar, i.e. $\frac{2}{2}$ time, (sometimes called ALLA BREVE time)

When I first came to this land

Duet

Traditional

On the repeat, omit these bars and go straight to the bar marked 2

Blowin' in the wind
Duet

Words and Music
by BOB DYLAN

Accompaniment for Keyboard
on samba rhythm setting

Play three times, then on to Chorus

4/4	Bb	Eb	F	Bb	Bb	Eb	F	F7

Chorus

Eb	F	Bb	Gm	Eb	F	Bb	Bb

The note B♭

The A key

Left thumb: press register key but do not cover hole

The FLAT lowers the pitch of a note by one semitone

HARMONY **Yo heave ho!**

Strongly

Traditional Russian song

The Key signature of F major

The flat on the middle line makes all the B's flat

Words and Music by
VERA MATSON
& ELVIS PRESLEY

Love me Tender

Caressingly

mp

B♭ accomp: E♭   F7   B♭7   E♭   E♭   G7   Cm   E♭7
C accomp: F   G7   C7   F   F   A7   Dm   F7

A♭   G7   C7   F7   B♭7   E♭
B♭   A7   D7   G7   C7   F

Low B♭

Cover left
thumb hole

Edelweiss

from *The Sound of Music*

Lyrics by OSCAR HAMMERSTEIN II
Music by RICHARD RODGERS

Semplice

| B♭ accomp: | E♭ | B♭ | E♭ | A♭ | E♭ | Cm | Fm | B♭7 |
| C accomp: | F | C | F | B♭ | F | Dm | Gm | C7 |

We wish you a merry Christmas

Traditional

Fast and jolly

■ Proceed to Low F on page 24; or dotted crotchet on page 25; or C♯ on page 27; or E♭ on page 30.

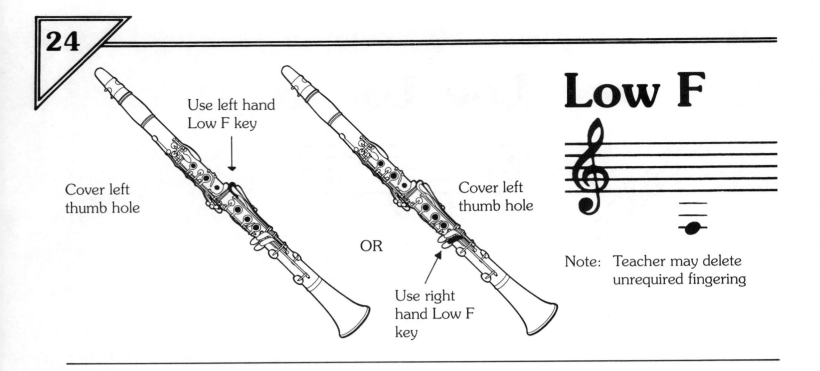

Low F

Cover left
thumb hole

Use left hand
Low F key

OR

Cover left
thumb hole

Use right
hand Low F
key

Note: Teacher may delete
unrequired fingering

Down to F

Scale and arpeggio of F major

Ode to joy

LUDWIG VAN BEETHOVEN
(1770-1827)

Allegro assai

mf

The dotted crotchet

Related ensemble material on page 49. *Auld lang syne* for flute unison on page 26 in the FLUTE book.

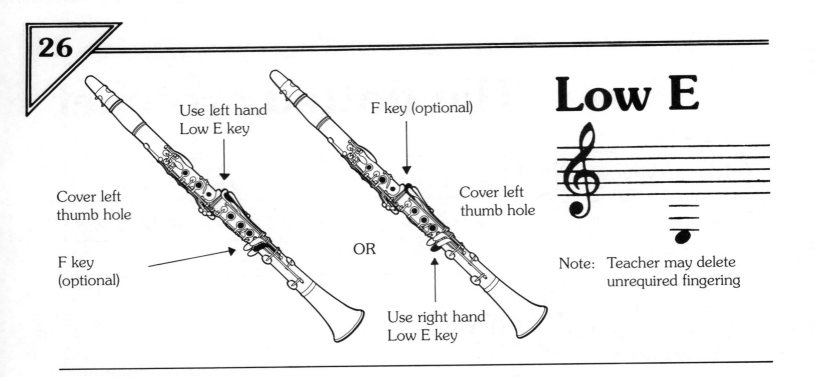

Low E

Note: Teacher may delete unrequired fingering

Down to E

Skip to my low E!

Traditional

God save the Queen

Traditional

■ Proceed to C♯ on page 27; or Upper Register on page 31; or Low F♯ on page 28.

The note C♯

The key signature of D major

Cover left thumb hole

C♯ key

Deck the halls

UNISON

Traditional

Lively

f

Rule Britannia

UNISON

THOMAS AUGUSTINE ARNE
(1710-1778)

Grandly

p (f)

■ Related ensemble material on page 37.

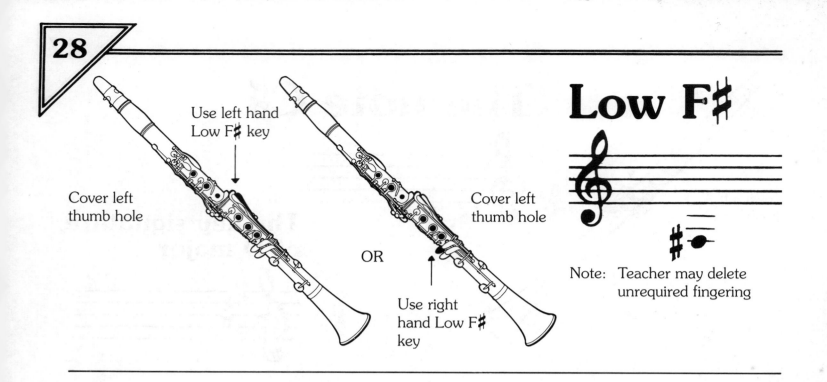

Low F♯

Note: Teacher may delete unrequired fingering

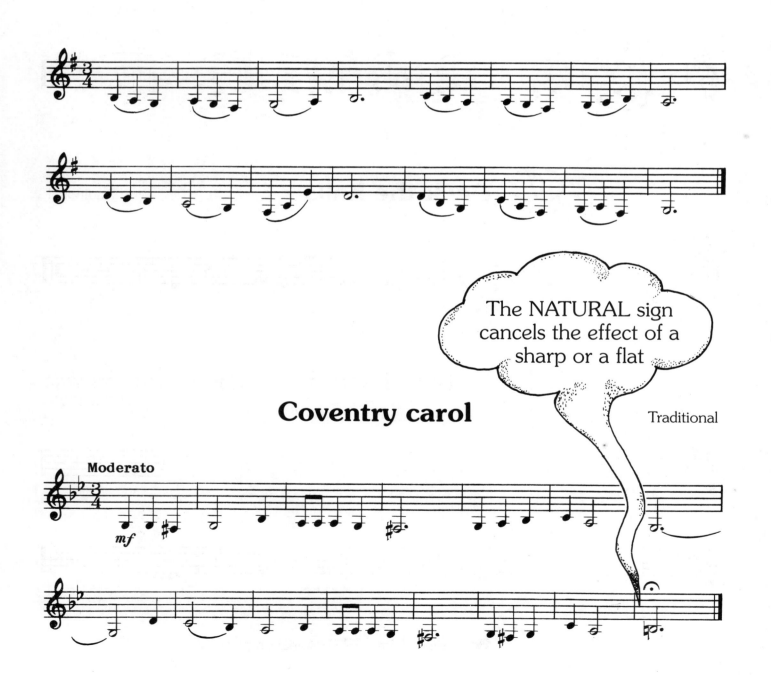

The NATURAL sign cancels the effect of a sharp or a flat

Coventry carol

Traditional

Moderato

mf

Low G♯ & A♭

Cover left thumb hole

Low G♯ key

Upper G♯ & A♭

No thumb

Upper G♯ key

The key signature of A major

Symphony No. 1

JOHANNES BRAHMS
(1833-1897)

Allegro non troppo

mf

Rigaudon

UNISON

HENRY PURCELL
(1659-1695)

Allegro

mp

f

Use right hand E and left hand F♯ here

The note E♭

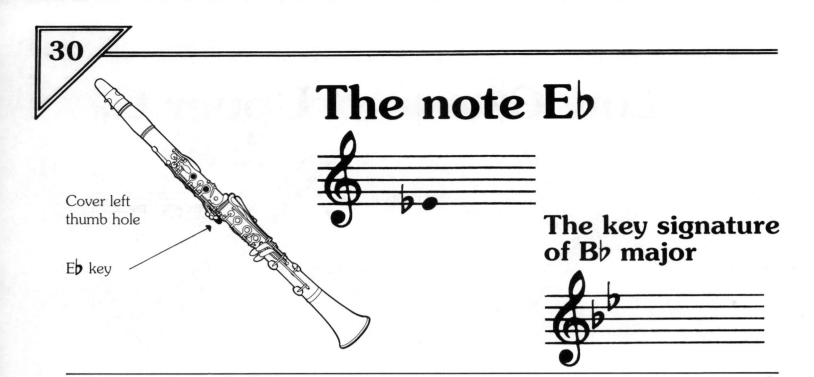

Cover left thumb hole

E♭ key

The key signature of B♭ major

Greensleeves

Traditional

Not fast, flowing

mp

mf

dim.

The upper register

For all these notes use the left thumb to press the register key and cover the left thumb hole at the same time

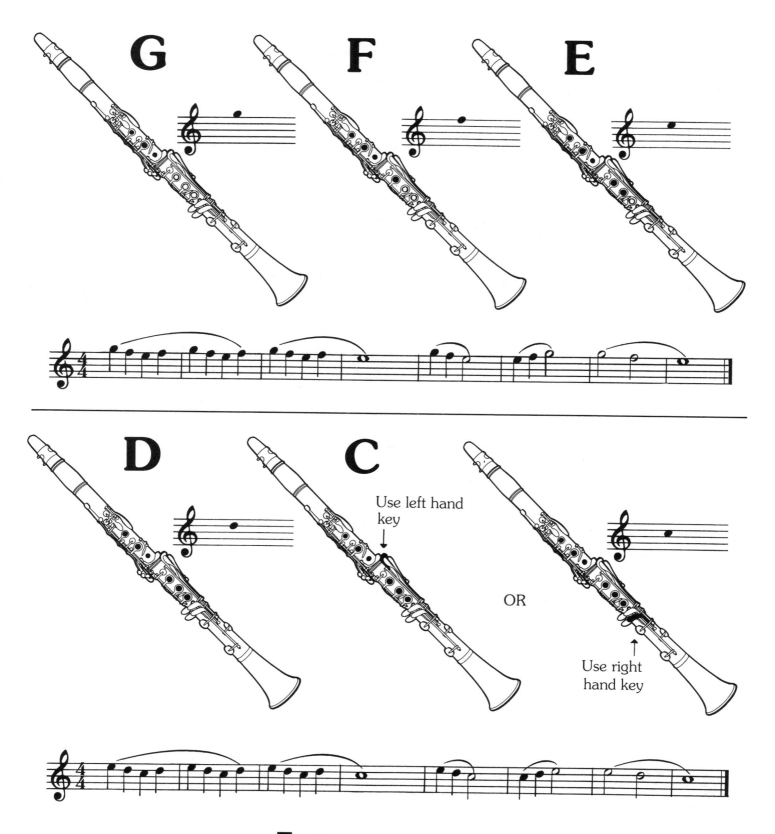

■ The two exercises on this page can be played together.

C, D, E, F and G together

Ode to joy

UNISON

LUDWIG VAN BEETHOVEN
(1770-1827)

Allegro assai

mf

■ The same piece appears on page 24 in the low register, with the same fingerings but without the register key.

When the saints go marching in

Traditional

Lively

f

play by ear

Brightly

Continue

Slowly

Continue

■ Proceed to High A on page 33; or Upper B on page 34.

High A

Cover left thumb hole and press register key

London bridge is falling down

Traditional

Not fast

mf

Twinkle, twinkle, little star

UNISON

Round

Traditional

Quite slowly

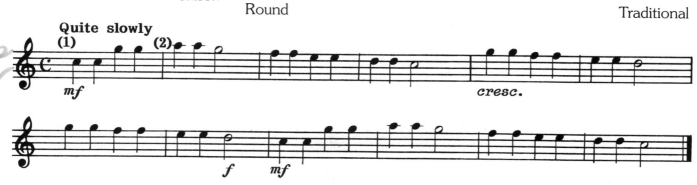

This old man

Traditional

Brightly

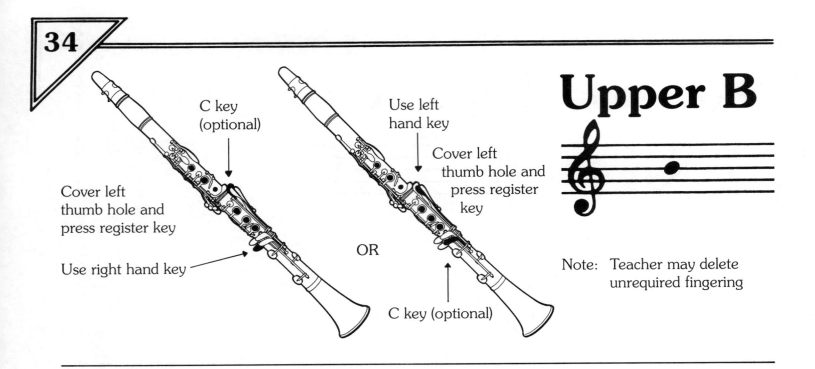

Upper B

Note: Teacher may delete unrequired fingering

Down to B

■ The above piece and *God save the Queen* appear on page 26 in the low register, with the same fingerings but without the register key.

God save the Queen

Traditional

UNISON

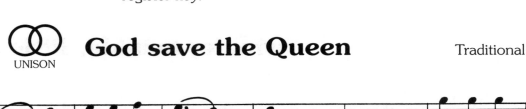

Don't sit under the apple tree

Words and Music by LEW BROWN
CHARLIE TOBIAS and SAM H. STEPT

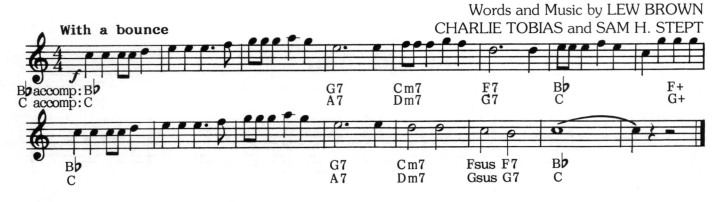

Joining the upper and lower registers

 UNISON

London's burning
Round

Traditional

Scale and arpeggio of G major

Wiegenlied
Traditional

Scale and arpeggio of F major

Victorian ballad

Morning has broken

Traditional

The first Nowell

Traditional

Polovtsian dance

ALEXANDER BORODIN
(1833-1887)

■ Related ensemble material on pages 37 & 39; proceed to
Upper F♯ or C♯ on page 38; or $\frac{6}{8}$ time on page 40.

Au clair de la lune

Traditional

Little donkey

Words and Music by
ERIC BOSWELL

The sharp, flat or natural sign appearing before a note is called an ACCIDENTAL. The sign affects all following notes of the SAME PITCH WITHIN THAT BAR. e.g. each C in this bar is sharp, not just the first one

■ Preparatory C♯ exercises on page 27.

Upper F♯ & G♭

Sing hosanna

Traditional

UNISON

Merrily

f

Upper C♯

The old hundredth

Traditional

Cover left thumb hole; press register key

Use LEFT hand key

RIGHT hand key

OR

Maestoso

f

■ $\frac{6}{8}$ time on page 40; Upper E♭ on page 41; high B and C on page 42.

6/8 time

and its relationship with 2/4 time

When Johnny comes marching home

Traditional

UNISON

play by ear

■ Related ensemble material on page 39; Upper E♮ on page 41; High B & C on page 42; *When Johnny colmes marching home* for flute unison on page 35 in the FLUTE book; quaver syncopation on page 44.

Upper E♭

E♭ key

Cover left
thumb hole
and press
register key

Away in a manger

WILLIAM JAMES KIRKPATRICK
(1838-1921)

Semplice
p

Scale and arpeggio of E♭ major

Villikins and his Dinah

Traditional

Moderately
mp   *mf*

f   *mf*

High B

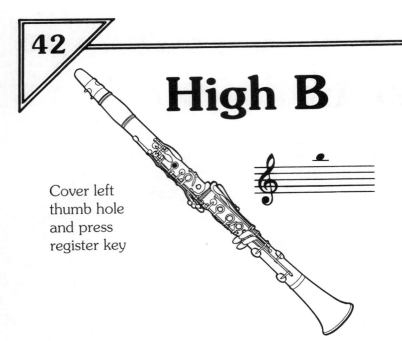

Cover left
thumb hole
and press
register key

High C

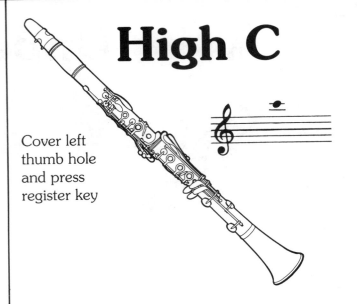

Cover left
thumb hole
and press
register key

Scale and arpeggio of C major

Pomp and Circumstance March No. 1

UNISON

EDWARD ELGAR
(1857-1934)

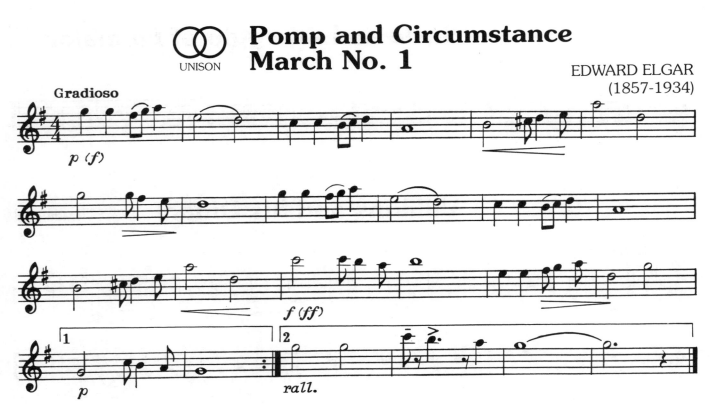

Gradioso

p (f)

f (ff)

1

2

p

rall.

Stranger on the shore

Words by ROBERT MELLIN
Music by ACKER BILK

Amazing grace

The QUAVER TRIPLET means that three quavers are played in the time of one crotchet

Traditional

Quaver syncopation

To be played:
(a) In strict time
(b) In swing time

Old Liza Jane

Bright and rhythmic

Caribbean dance

UNISON

Tempo di rumba

Fine

D.C. al Fine

■ Syncopated crotchets on pages 15 & 21; Related ensemble material on page 39; *Caribbean dance* for flute unison on page 43 in the FLUTE book.

Simply blue

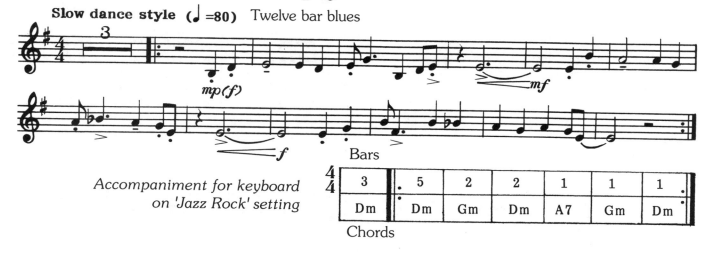

Slow dance style (♩=80) Twelve bar blues

Accompaniment for keyboard on 'Jazz Rock' setting

Bars

4/4	3	. 5	2	2	1	1	1 .
Chords	Dm	Dm	Gm	Dm	A7	Gm	Dm

West Indian carnival

Fast and jolly

Semiquavers in $\frac{2}{4}$

Semiquavers are sometimes called SIXTEENTH-NOTES

Slowly

Semiquaver study

UNISON

Related ensemble material on pages 48 & 55.

The dotted quaver

Say 'goodbye'
from *The Marriage of Figaro*

Allegro

WOLFGANG AMADEUS MOZART (1756-1791)

John Brown's body

Traditional

Marziale

play by ear

Fast and jolly   Joyfully

Continue   Continue

Related ensemble material on page 55.

Michael row the boat ashore

Traditional

Canzona

ADRIANO BANCHIERI (1568-1634)

Compose an accompaniment for tambour using crotchets, quavers and semi-quavers

■ Because the *Canzona* is a four-part polyphonic piece, the parts above cannot be played simply as a clarinet duet. Third and fourth parts are to be found, however, in all other TEAM WOODWIND books.

O Little Town of Bethlehem

Traditional

St. Anthony chorale

JOSEPH HAYDN (1732-1809)

High A♭ & G♯

Cover left thumb hole and press register key

A♭ /G♯ key

High B♭

Cover left thumb hole and press register key

B♭ key

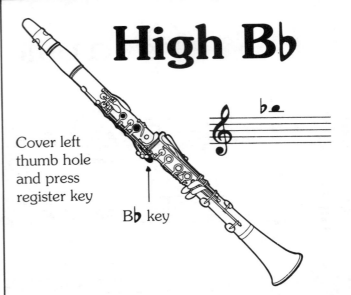

Frère Jacques

Traditional

Brightly

(1) (2) (3) (4)

f

The Pink Panther

by HENRY MANCINI

Slyly

pp

B♭accomp: B♭m
C accomp: Cm

F♯7
A♭7

B♭m
Cm

ff

B7
C♯7

B♭m
Cm

F♯7
A♭7

ff

B♭m NC
Cm

B♭m
Cm

F♯7
A♭7

B♭m
Cm

ppp

B♭m/maj7
Cm/maj7

ff

Trio

from *Symphony No. 39*

WOLFGANG AMADEUS MOZART
(1756-1791)

Scarboro' fair

Traditional

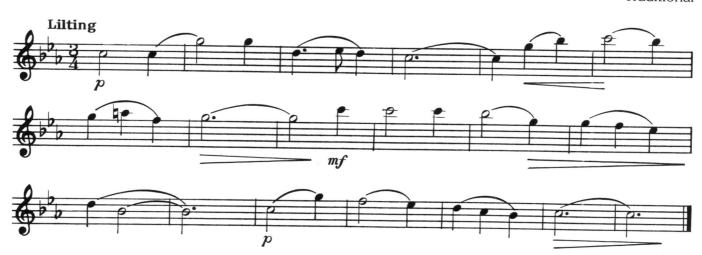

Chromatic scale of F

High D

Cover left thumb hole and press register key

E♮ key

Star Wars Main Title

by JOHN WILLIAMS

UNISON

High C♯

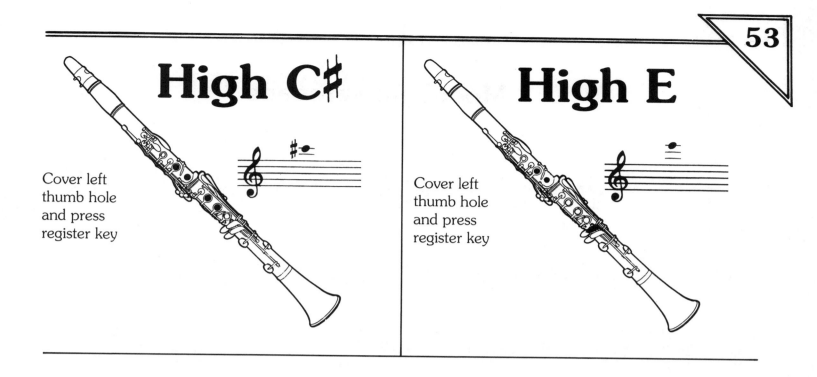

Cover left
thumb hole
and press
register key

High E

Cover left
thumb hole
and press
register key

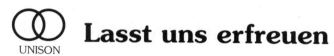

UNISON

Lasst uns erfreuen

Traditional

I gave my love a cherry

Traditional

Moonlight serenade

Words by MITCHELL PARISH
Music by GLENN MILLER

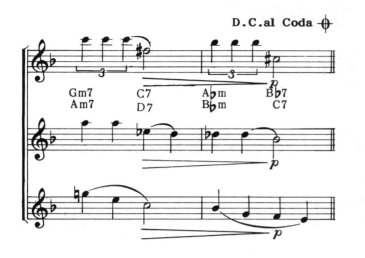

March

from *Judas Maccabaeus*

GEORGE FRIDERIC HANDEL (1685-1759)

Scales and arpeggios

Scale and arpeggio of C major

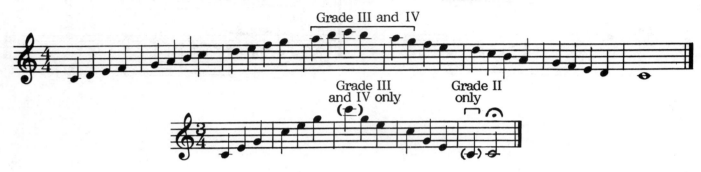

Scale and arpeggio of F major

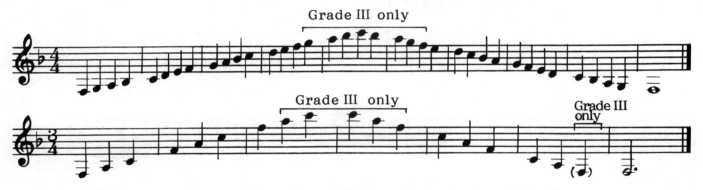

Scale and arpeggio of G major

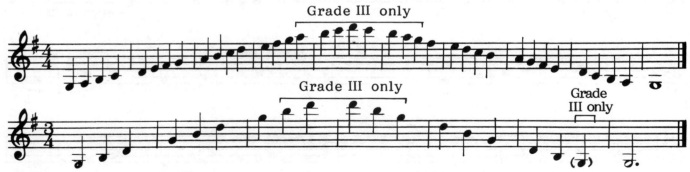

Scale and arpeggio of B♭ major

Scale and arpeggio of D major

Scale and arpeggio of A major

Scale of A minor harmonic

Arpeggio of A minor

Scale of D minor harmonic

Grade III and IV

Arpeggio of D minor

Grade III and IV

Grade II only

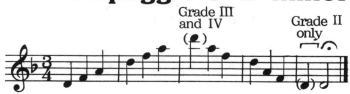

Scale of E minor harmonic

Arpeggio of E minor

Scale of G minor harmonic

Arpeggio of G minor

Scale of B minor harmonic

Arpeggio of B minor

Scale of C minor harmonic

Arpeggio of C minor

Sweet Georgia Brown

Words and Music by
BEN BERNIE,
KENNETH CASEY,
MACEO PINKARD

The theme (up to FINE) can be played in unison with FLUTE.

Minuet

WOLFGANG AMADEUS MOZART
(1756-1791)

from *Divertimento No. 4*

UNISON

Over the rainbow

Words by E. Y. HARBURG
Music by HAROLD ARLEN

L. A. Nitespot

Twelve bar blues

Fine

You can improvise
using the notes of
the 'Blues Scale'

Accompaniment for keyboard
on 'Slow Rock' setting

Bars					
4	2	2	1	1	2
C	F	C	G	F	C

Chords

12/99